Information and Communication Technology

KEY STAGE 2:
YEAR 3
PRIMARY 4

Frances Mackay

HOPSCOTCH
EDUCATIONAL PUBLISHING

Contents

ABOUT THE SERIES

Developing ICT Skills is a series of books written specifically to complement the QCA and DfEE *Information Technology Scheme of Work for Key Stages 1 and 2*. There is one book for each year from Reception/Year 1 (Scottish Primary 1/2), through Key Stage 1 to Year 6 (Scottish Primary 7) at the end of Key Stage 2.

The series offers a structured approach with the non-specialist in mind and provides detailed lesson plans to teach specific ICT skills. A unique feature of the series is the provision of differentiated photocopiable activities designed to support each lesson. Most of these activities are independent tasks that can be completed away from the computer or ICT equipment being used, thereby enabling the teacher to work with a focus group at the computer. The differentiation of the activities considerably reduces teacher preparation time when planning group work.

The lessons have been specifically written for the classroom with access to only one computer but will, of course, work equally well in a computer suite situation.

Accompanying each of the two books for Key Stage 1 is a CD-Rom, produced by AirCom International, that contains activities designed to support each lesson. Schools will not, therefore, need a separate word processor, art or music package, for example, to teach the ICT skills being addressed. If schools prefer to use their own computer programs, however, the books are designed to stand alone without the accompanying CD-Rom.

ABOUT THIS BOOK

This book is for teachers of Year 3 (Scottish Primary level 4) children. It aims to:

✦ develop children's ICT skills through a series of structured lessons aimed at increasing children's awareness of the strengths and limitations of ICT;

✦ support teachers by providing practical teaching methods and activity ideas based on whole-class, group, paired and individual teaching;

✦ support non-specialist teachers by providing structured lesson plans with practical ideas and 'specialist tips' designed to address some of the common problems the children (and teachers!) may experience;

✦ provide lessons that are cross-curricular wherever possible;

✦ encourage the children to recognise the importance of ICT in everyday experiences;

✦ encourage enjoyment as well as confidence in using ICT skills.

LESSON CONTENT

Learning objectives

This sets out the specific learning objectives for each lesson.

Resources

This is a list of what you will need to do the lessons.

Whole class introduction

This provides ideas for introducing the activity, and may include key questions to ask the children, so that they can move on to their group task having learned concepts and the vocabulary they will need for the group activities.

Group activities

Focus group – with the teacher
This follows the whole class introduction and is a teaching session with the teacher working together with the children at the computer (or other ICT equipment). The teaching in this session can either be carried out with the class as a whole (by using a computer and a projected screen or by using a computer suite) or within a small group while the rest of the class do the photocopiable activity sheets (if appropriate) or another (sometimes related) independent task. This section contains suggestions for teaching the key concepts and skills relating directly to the ICT learning objectives for the lesson. Hints and tips are provided to help support the teacher when introducing these skills.

Using the photocopiable activity sheets
The activity sheets provide three activities that can be done more or less independently from the teacher. These sheets are differentiated so that the same task can be completed by below average, average and above average children at their own level. Activity sheet 1 tasks are the easiest and activity sheet 3 the hardest. In most cases, the sheets contain tasks that are designed to be completed away from the computer or ICT equipment being used but reinforce the skills that will be used at the computer itself. Many activities are also designed so the children can compare a manual task with a computer one (editing text, for example), thereby enabling a discussion during the plenary session about the strengths and limitations of ICT.

Sometimes, the sheets can be completed immediately after the whole class introduction (so some children may be working with the teacher in a small group at the computer while the rest are completing the sheets). At other times, the sheets are to be completed only after the children have experienced the focus group session (in a classroom with only one computer, the children may need to be set other independent tasks until they have been part of the focus group).

For each lesson, then, each child should experience the whole class introduction and a focus group session as well as completing an activity sheet. In classrooms with only one computer this means the teacher may need to organise the lesson over a week, for example:

Mon	whole class introduction
	group A – with the teacher at computer (focus group session)
	groups B, C and D – completing activity sheets
Tues	group B – focus group session
	group A – activity sheet
	groups C and D – independent tasks
Wed	group C – focus group session
	groups A, B and D – independent tasks
Thurs	group D – focus group session
	groups A, B and C – independent tasks
	plenary – all groups

 Plenary session

This suggests ideas for a whole-class review to discuss the learning outcomes, and gives questions to ask so that children have a chance to reflect on what they have learned and for the teacher to assess their knowledge and understanding. This session may not necessarily take place on the same day as the whole class introduction - it may come at the end of the week after all the children have completed their focus group session and activity sheets.

 APPENDIX

At the back of this book are some extra photocopiable pages. Page 54 offers suggestions for how these pages could be used. Most of the pages have been prepared for the teacher to use as resources for particular lessons but there are also ideas on how to use the pages to develop further activities in follow-up sessions. Where relevant, these pages also contain the answers to particular activity sheets.

Page 64 contains an assessment sheet that outlines the basic concepts and skills that a Year 3 child should experience. The teacher can photocopy this page for each child and, together with the work produced from each lesson, use it to compile a comprehensive individual ICT profile to make assessments and determine future targets.

 **HARDWARE REQUIREMENTS**

Teachers using this book will require a Windows-based multi-media computer and colour printer as well as several tape recorders.

SOFTWARE REQUIREMENTS

- ✦ a WYSIWYG (What You See Is What You Get) word processor with a graphic insert capability;
- ✦ a CD-Rom with pictures or a clip art file;
- ✦ a graphics package or desk-top publishing program;
- ✦ a CD-Rom of musical instruments;
- ✦ music composition software with icons to represent musical phrases;
- ✦ a computer database;
- ✦ a computer simulation that allows the user to make choices, enter data and explore consequences;
- ✦ e-mail facility.

If you do not have all the software listed, contact your LEA for a recommended software toolbox. They may also provide technical support and training. Alternatively, contact Granada Learning on 0161 827 2927 (Blackcat Toolbox) or Logotron on 01223 425558.

TEACHING ICT

For many of today's adults there has always been a degree of mystique surrounding ICT skills. Some people have even avoided contact with computers altogether! However, in the teaching profession, this is not an option. In truth, there is nothing difficult about acquiring or teaching ICT and, in fact, there has never been a better or more exciting time to become a computer user. To become a confident ICT user, whether teacher or pupil, you need to be taught a few basic skills and to become familiar with the way technology works, but you do not need to become an expert. The National Curriculum requires ICT to be taught to all pupils and this can seem daunting if the teacher is learning alongside the pupils. In this series we aim to provide the teacher with the materials, skills and knowledge that will make covering the ICT Scheme of Work an achievable and positive experience. We expect children who take part in the lessons to learn age-appropriate ICT skills and to become discerning users of technology.

Schools that teach ICT skills discretely then transfer those skills to other subject areas find that children achieve higher levels of ICT competence than when ICT skills are taught **only** through other subjects. This suggests that teachers should set aside time specifically for the teaching of ICT skills. This does not mean that it is necessary to timetable ICT lessons every week but it is important to make sure some ICT lessons are devoted to the teaching of specific ICT skills. This can be carried out through occasional whole-class lessons as well as small group or individual lessons and does not necessarily require the whole class to be working on ICT at the same time. The lessons in this book agree with this premise and ICT is the main focus of each one. However, where there are opportunities for links with other curriculum areas, advantage of this has been taken.

Prior to the publication of the QCA and DfEE IT SOW it was difficult for schools to know exactly what ICT skills should be taught to each year group. We have now been

presented with a clear and comprehensive guide which clearly demonstrates continuity and progression. If you are working with older children who have not had the opportunity to acquire the rudimentary skills, it would be best to work at the correct level for these children. Hence the years and levels suggested in the IT SOW and in this series of books are to be taken as desirable guidelines.

In order to achieve a high level of success for the children, teaching intentions should be very clear and built within a whole-school scheme of work that demonstrates evident continuity and progression of concepts and skills. This is extremely important in ICT because today, perhaps more than ever before, children vary considerably in their ICT capabilities. Many children who have access to ICT outside school can appear to have greater skills in handling software and hardware but teachers need to be aware that these children may not necessarily have the full range of ICT capabilities expected of them in the programmes of study. Regular observations and assessments are therefore necessary to ascertain the best tasks and experiences to support the children's learning.

Reliability of the technology has often been one of the biggest hurdles for schools! Therefore, before you begin to use the lessons in this series, we recommend that you check that all the necessary equipment is working correctly. Access to broken or out-of-date technology is time wasting and very frustrating for teachers and children alike.

Published by Hopscotch Educational Publishing Ltd,
29 Waterloo Place, Leamington Spa CV32 5LA.
(Tel: 01926 744227)
© 1999 Hopscotch Educational Publishing

Written by Frances Mackay
Series consultant – Ayleen Driver
Series design by Blade Communications
Illustrated by Ann Biggs and Tony O'Donnell
Cover illustration by Susan Hutchison
Printed by Clintplan, Southam

Our thanks go to the Marine Biological Association in Plymouth for their help with our marine database information.

'The Cliff-top' is by Robert Bridges from *The Shorter Poems of Robert Bridges*.

Every effort has been made to obtain permission for copyright material. The publishers would be grateful for any discrepancy to be notified.

ISBN 1-902239-42-3

Lesson 1

Using fonts

 ### Learning objectives

◆ To explore calligrams.
◆ To understand that typefaces can be used to create different effects.
◆ To alter font type, size and colour in a word processing program to create an effect.
◆ To manipulate text to create different effects.

 ### Resources

◆ Photocopiable page 55.
◆ A word processing program, preferably one that allows text to be manipulated.

 ### Whole class introduction

◆ Enlarge the poem 'Creatures of the Sea' (page 55) on a photocopier. Share it with the children. What do they notice that is different about this poem compared with most other poems they have read? Explain that when the formation of the letters or the type of font used reflect the meaning of the poem, it is called a calligram.
◆ Discuss how the poet has created the different effects, for example how the word 'big' is typed in big letters. Which word do the children think is most effective? Why? How effective do they think this approach to writing a poem is? Does it make the poem more interesting to look at and read? Talk about how colour could also be used if the poem was a colour reproduction.
◆ Ask the children to suggest other instances where using text to create special effects might be useful – advertising posters or book covers, for example.
◆ Ask them to suggest some ideas of their own for making words look like their meaning. Ask them to try out these words: tall, grow, scary, tiny, jump, smile and red. Share their responses. Ask some of them to draw their ideas on the board.
◆ Tell the children that they are going to try out some more ideas of their own by writing a calligram using an activity sheet and that you will also be showing them how to create special text effects using the computer.

 ### Group activities

Focus group – with the teacher

◆ Photocopy the poem 'The Cliff-Top' on page 55 and glue it on to card. Show the children the font editing features on the word processor. Explain how to change the font type, size and colour. If possible, show them other text manipulation features, such as how to make wavy or shaped letters.
◆ Then ask them to work in pairs to set out the poem as a calligram by deciding which words in the poem can be made to look like their meaning. Explain that they may not be able to create as wide a range of effects as in 'Creatures of the Sea' because they are limited by the capabilities of the word processor they are using. Tell them that you want them to concentrate on creating different font type, size and colour effects. Print out their results.

Using the photocopiable activity sheets

◆ The sheets can be used before or after the computer session.

 ### Plenary session

Share the responses to the activity sheets. How many different effects could be created for the same words? Which words were easy to do? Which words were difficult? Why? Share the calligram produced using the computer. Did the children experience any difficulties? How did they overcome them? Which method was easier to use – pen and paper or word processor? Why? Which method could create a wider range of effects? Which method provides better presentation? What other uses can the children suggest for using the word processor in this way?

✦ A sea poem ✦

✦ Read this poem about waves.

Waves

Big waves, little waves,
Green waves and blue.
I like to skip along the shore
And dip my toes in you!

✦ Make these words from the poem look like their meaning. The first one has been done for you.

big　　　　　　**BIG**

little

green

blue

skip

wave

toes

✦ A sea poem ✦

✦ Read this poem about waves.

Waves

Big blue waves come crashing
Upon the golden shore.
I love to watch them leaving
And return to me once more.

✦ Rewrite the poem as a calligram by making some of the words look like their meaning, for example:

Big **BIG**

✦ A sea poem ✦

✦ Read this poem about waves. Then rewrite it as a calligram by making some of the words look like their meaning.

Waves

Huge waves grow like magic
As they hasten to the shore.
White foam glistens like diamonds
As they spread across the floor.
In a never-ending cycle
Blue waves return once more.

✦ Rewrite the poem here.

Lesson 2

Using the shift key

 Learning objectives

✦ To reinforce understanding of speech punctuation and the use of question and exclamation marks.
✦ To use the shift key in a word processing program to type characters and capital letters.

 Resources

✦ Photocopiable page 56.
✦ A word processing program.

 Whole class introduction

✦ Enlarge page 56. Explain to the children that you are going to look at the way speech is used in stories. Share the first half of the story with them, making sure they can all see the text. How can they tell which parts in the story are words spoken by the children? Use the text to revise speech marks and remind them that the marks go around only the actual words spoken by the characters. Remind them about the use of capital letters and how a new line is used every time a new person speaks. Point out the question and exclamation marks. Ask the children to tell you when they are used. Discuss how this affects the way we read the text.

✦ Now look at the second part of the text (underneath the illustration). What do the children notice that is different? Is this text difficult to read? What things are missing? Work through the text together deciding where the speech marks, commas, capital letters, question marks and exclamation marks should go. Read the text again.

✦ Ask the children to suggest what they think might happen next in the story. What might be inside the box? Where might it have come from? Why was it on the beach?

✦ Explain that they will be able to find out by doing the next activity. Tell them they will be reading the next part of the story as well as putting in the speech marks and other punctuation. Explain that you will also be showing them how to use the computer to do the same task.

 Group activities

Focus group - with the teacher

✦ Before the lesson, enter some text where the speech marks are missing. (You might like to enter three short texts – one with only speech marks missing, one with speech, question and exclamation marks missing and one with capital letters also missing). Remind the children how to use the shift key to make capital letters. Tell them that the shift key can also be used to type other things. Show them where the exclamation mark, question mark and speech mark are on the key board. Show them how to hold down the shift key and press another key at the same time. Let each child have a turn at this.

✦ Open the file with the prepared text and explain to the children what you want them to do. Demonstrate how to use the mouse or cursor keys to position the cursor and how to add in the missing characters. Then ask them to work in pairs to complete the text and print out their work.

Using the photocopiable activity sheets

✦ The activity sheets should be used before the children use the computer.

 Plenary session

Share the responses to the activity sheets. Does everyone agree where the punctuation should go? Share the responses to the computer text. Did they have any problems? Ask the children to consider the advantages and disadvantages of using the computer to perform this task.

You may want to encourage the children to write their own endings to the 'Buried treasure' story.

✦ Buried treasure ✦

✦ Read the next part of the Buried Treasure story below.
  Decide where all the speech marks go and put them in.

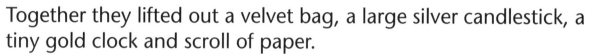

Tamal and Anna peered into the box.

Wow!   exclaimed Anna.

Let's take them out,   said Tamal.

Together they lifted out a velvet bag, a large silver candlestick, a tiny gold clock and scroll of paper.

I wonder what's inside the bag,   said Anna.

Here, let me help you with it,   said Frank.

Frank carefully opened the velvet bag and tipped the contents out on the work bench. They couldn't believe what they saw.

There on the bench was the most beautiful collection of jewellery they had ever seen.

It must be worth a fortune,   said Tamal.

Where do you think it came from?   asked Anna.

We've got to report this to the police!   exclaimed Frank.

While Frank went to the phone, Tamal opened the paper scroll. It was a plan of a large house.

Look at this,   he said.   It's a plan of some sort.

Yes,   agreed Anna.   And look at the name there. It's Osborn House, just down the road.

I think we've uncovered something really important,   said Tamal. I hope there's a big reward!

✦ Buried treasure ✦

✦ Read the next part of the Buried treasure story below. Decide where all the speech marks, question marks and exclamation marks go. Put them in.

Tamal and Anna peered into the box.

Wow   exclaimed Anna.

Let's take them out, said Tamal.

Together they lifted out a velvet bag, a large silver candlestick, a tiny gold clock and scroll of paper.

What do you think is inside the bag   asked Anna.

Here, let me help you with it,   said Frank.

Frank carefully opened the velvet bag and tipped the contents out on the work bench. They couldn't believe what they saw. There on the bench was the most beautiful collection of jewellery they had ever seen.

It must be worth a fortune,   said Tamal.

Where do you think it came from   asked Anna.

We've got to report this to the police   exclaimed Frank.

While Frank went to the phone, Tamal opened the paper scroll. It was a plan of a large house.

Look at this,   he said.   It's a plan of some sort.

Yes, agreed Anna.   And look at the name there. It's Osborn House, just down the road.

I think we've uncovered something really important, said Tamal.   I hope there's a big reward

ICT Skills

✦ Buried treasure ✦

✦ Read the next part of the Buried treasure story below. Decide where all the speech marks, question marks, exclamation marks and capital letters go. Put them in.

tamal and anna peered into the box.

wow exclaimed anna.

let's take them out,   said tamal.

together they lifted out a velvet bag, a large silver candlestick, a tiny gold clock and scroll of paper.

what do you think is inside the bag   asked anna.

here, let me help you with it,   said frank.

frank carefully opened the velvet bag and tipped the contents out on the work bench. they couldn't believe what they saw.

there on the bench was the most beautiful collection of jewellery they had ever seen.

it must be worth a fortune,   said tamal.

where do you think it came from   asked anna.

we've got to report this to the police   exclaimed frank.

while frank went to the phone, tamal opened the paper scroll. It was a plan of a large house.

look at this, he said.   it's a plan of some sort.

yes,   agreed anna.   and look at the name there. it's osborn house, just down the road.

i think we've uncovered something really important, said tamal. i hope there's a big reward

Lesson 3

Editing text

 Learning objectives

- To experiment with substituting adjectives to improve text.
- To understand that ICT can be used to alter text to improve it.
- To amend text in a word processing program using highlighting and over-typing.
- To save changes to work.

 Resources

- Photocopiable page 57.
- A word processing program.

 Whole class introduction

- Enlarge page 57. Tell the children that they are going to look at adjectives. Ask them to remind you what adjectives are. Explain how adjectives can describe a noun. Tell them how important adjectives can be in helping us describe things in detail. Write up some simple examples, such as 'The fish has a fin.' Rewrite the sentences using adjectives, such as 'The fish has a beautiful yellow fin.' Discuss how the adjectives help us to provide a more informative and interesting description of the fish. Ask the children to think of other adjectives they know. List them on the board. Use them in sentences.

- Now look together at the sentences about sharks on page 57. Can the children find the adjectives in each sentence? Underline them. Can they suggest other adjectives to describe a shark? Ask them to make up some suitable sentences.

- Say that sometimes we can over-use the same adjective in our writing. Use the writing about 'The whale' on page 57 as an example. Explain that in this example, the word 'big' has been used too often and that the text could be greatly improved if we replaced this word with different adjectives. Read through the text together and ask the children to suggest which words in the boxes could be used to replace the underlined words. Make sure they realise that the replacement word must be an appropriate one.

 Group activities

Focus group – with the teacher

- Before the lesson, enter some text where an adjective such as 'nice', 'good' or 'small' has been over-used. Read the text together. Show the children how to use the mouse to highlight a word in the text and over-type it to change it. Discuss why we might want to do this, for example after we have written a story, we may want to improve it or we may have made a mistake and want to correct it. Tell them that in this case the text has an adjective in it that has been over-used. Can they tell you the word? Explain that you want them to highlight and over-type this word throughout the text and replace it with a variety of more interesting or appropriate adjectives. Suggest they use a thesaurus (in book form or as a facility of the word processor). Demonstrate how to save their work and give it a sensible name. Ask the children to print out their work.
Note: Not all word processors have an easily accessible over-typing facility so you may need to highlight, delete, then type in the new word. Also remember that when the children save their work, it will replace the file you loaded, so keep a copy of the original on disc or in another directory.

Using the photocopiable activity sheets

- Use the activity sheets before using the computer.

 Plenary session

Share the responses to the activity sheets. Does everyone agree with the words selected? Have the sentences been improved by using more interesting/appropriate adjectives? Share the responses to the computer task. Did anyone have any problems? Compare editing work on paper with using a computer – which one is easier? Why? Which one provides better final presentation? What are the advantages and disadvanatges of using a computer to doing writing tasks?

✦ Dolphins ✦

✦ Read the sentences about dolphins below.
Underline the <u>adjective</u> in each one.

1. Dolphins are beautiful.

2. Dolphins have round snouts.

3. They breathe through a small hole on their heads.

4. Dolphins have sharp teeth.

5. Dolphins make strange sounds.

✦ Choose words from the box or some of your own to
replace the word 'good' in these sentences. Cross out the
word 'good' and write the word you have chosen above it.

1. Dolphins are good swimmers.

2. They have a good nature.

3. Dolphins have a good brain.

4. Dolphins are good hunters.

5. People watch dolphins in good weather.

| fair |
| friendly |
| great |
| calm |
| clever |
| excellent |
| fine |
| pleasant |
| expert |

✦ Dolphins ✦

✦ Read the sentences about dolphins below.
Underline the two <u>adjectives</u> in each one.

1. Dolphins are wonderful, friendly creatures.
2. They have smooth round snouts.
3. They breathe through a tiny blowhole at the top of their sleek heads.
4. Dolphins have strong jaws and sharp teeth.
5. Dolphins make weird sounds and high whistles.
6. Dolphins are able to make long dives into deep water.
7. Some types of dolphins live in large groups and others live in small groups.
8. Dolphins have grey shiny bodies.

✦ Use a thesaurus to help you replace the word 'good' in all of these sentences with a different word. Cross out 'good' and rewrite your own word in its place.

1. Dolphins are good swimmers.

2. They have a good nature.

3. Dolphins have a good brain.

4. Dolphins are good hunters.

5. People like to watch dolphins in good weather.

✦ Dolphins ✦

✦ Read the paragraph below about dolphins.
How many <u>adjectives</u> can you find?
Underline them.

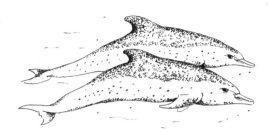

Dolphins are aquatic mammals. They are different from porpoises
because they have round snouts and conical teeth. The porpoise
has a blunt snout and a fatter body. The buffeo dolphin is small and
graceful (1.2 metres) and the largest is the bottle-nose dolphin
(3 metres). Dolphins are fast swimmers. This is because they have
streamlined bodies. They use their strong jaws and sharp teeth to
catch fish. Like whales, dolphins breathe through a tiny blowhole at
the top of their smooth heads. Some types of dolphins, such as the
Pacific white-sided dolphin, live in large groups.

✦ Use a thesaurus to help you replace the word 'good' in the paragraph
below. Cross out 'good' each time and rewrite your own word in its place.

Dolphins are good swimmers. They have a good nature and

are good to humans. They have a good brain and can be

taught to do good things. Dolphins are good hunters and

can catch good numbers of fish. They use their good strong

teeth to catch the fish. People like to watch dolphins in

good weather.

ICT Skills
Year 3/P4

ICT
Skills

Photocopiable
©Hopscotch Educational Publishing
17

Lesson 4

Using text and graphics

 Learning objectives

+ To understand that text and graphics can be combined to communicate information.
+ To combine text and graphics (involving copy, paste, insert, alignment and re-sizing of a graphic) in a word processor capable of doing this or a desk-top publishing program.

 Resources

+ Photocopiable page 58.
+ Picture dictionaries and information books.
+ A word processor/desk-top publishing program and a CD-Rom with pictures or a clip art file.

 Whole class introduction

+ Enlarge page 58. Cut it in half and cut out the four pictures at the bottom of the page. Tell the children that they will be looking at information books. Show them a picture dictionary. Ask them to tell you what is different about this dictionary compared with an ordinary one. Why does it use illustrations? How does it help us understand the information on the page? Do the children use illustrations to help them understand things better? Remind them how they used pictures to help them when they first learned to read.
+ Show them some information books where the illustration/photograph really enhances the text, such as a picture of a machine that is being described or a photograph of an unfamiliar animal. Discuss how the use of pictures enables us to understand the text more fully as well as providing further information not mentioned in the text.
+ Share page 58. Read through the text together. Would the text be improved with pictures? Ask the children to look carefully at the four pictures to decide which should go with each piece of text. Agree and glue them in place. Have the pictures improved the page and helped them understand the text more? Tell them that they will be exploring pictures and text further using an activity sheet and a computer program.

 Group activities

Focus group – with the teacher

+ Before the lesson, enter some pieces of text that would be enhanced by illustrations. Explain the term 'graphic' and how a computer can be used to combine pictures and writing to produce a finished page similar to a poster or a page in a book or magazine/newspaper. Demonstrate how to locate, copy and paste and/or insert a graphic into a piece of text. Show them how to re-size the graphic so that it becomes larger or smaller to suit their needs. Demonstrate how to use align right, align left and centre to alter the position of the text (if appropriate) to create the desired outcome.
+ Ask them to work in pairs to locate graphics and copy them into the text, then print out their work. It may be useful to write the instructions down to help them remember what to do.
  Note: in any Windows-operating system, you can cut and paste across a variety of programs. For example, if you want to take an image from an art package, select the image (or part of the image), go to edit and choose copy. Then open the word processor, go to edit and choose paste.

Using the photocopiable activity sheets

+ The sheets could be used before or after the computer session.

 Plenary session

Share the responses to the activity sheets. Can other information be learned from the pictures that is not mentioned in the text? Do the pictures help us to understand the information better? Compare this cutting and pasting activity with the computer task. Which was easier to do? Which one gives us more opportunities to alter the way it is presented? What other uses can the children suggest for using this program? How useful is it? How useful are the pictures/clip art?

✦ Ships and boats ✦

✦ Read the information below. Cut out the pictures at the bottom of the page. Decide which pictures belong to each piece of writing. Colour them in. Glue them in place.

Tanker

A tanker is a very big ship. It has a very long flat deck. It is used to carry large amounts of liquid cargo such as oil.

Submarine

A submarine is a boat that can go on or under the water. It uses special tanks filled with water to make it sink. Some submarines can travel under water for many months.

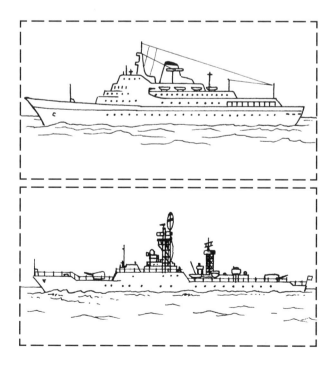

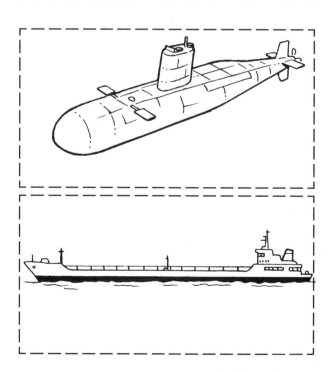

✦ Ships and boats ✦

✦ Read the information below. Cut out the pictures at the bottom of the page. Decide which pictures belong to each piece of writing. Stick them in place.

Paddle steamer

A paddle steamer is a ship propelled by large paddles that are turned by a steam engine. Paddle steamers can be used to carry cargo or passengers.

Barge

A barge is a flat-bottomed boat used to carry cargo especially on canals. A long pole can be used to propel the barge.

Dinghy

A dinghy is a small, open boat that can be powered by sails, oars or an outboard motor.

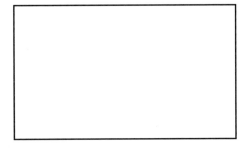

ICT Skills

✦ Ships and boats ✦

✦ Read the information below. Cut out the pictures at the bottom of the page. Decide which pictures belong to each piece of writing. Glue them in place.

Kayak

A kayak is a canoe-like boat with a covered-in frame. The frame can be wooden with a canvas cover or be made of fibreglass.

Schooner

A schooner is a sailing boat with at least two masts, rigged fore and aft.

Frigate

A frigate is a warship that is used mainly to defend other ships against enemy submarines. It is smaller than a destroyer.

Aircraft carrier

An aircraft carrier is the largest and most powerful warship. It has a flight deck for planes to land on.

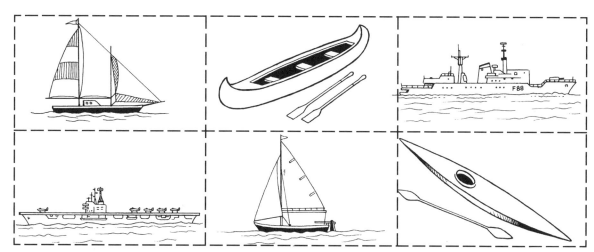

Lesson 5

Recording sounds

 Learning objectives

♦ To understand that sounds can be recorded and stored.
♦ To use ICT to locate and record sounds.

 Resources

♦ Photocopiable page 59 or pictures of musical instrument families.
♦ Tape recorders.
♦ Percussion instruments (as in the activity sheets).
♦ A CD-Rom of musical instruments.

 Whole class introduction

♦ Use the pictures of musical instruments on photocopiable page 59 to initiate a discussion about musical instrument families. How many of the instruments are the children familiar with? Can any of them play some of these instruments? Use the CD-Rom of musical instruments to demonstrate the sounds made by some of them. You could do this as a game: guess what family it belongs to; guess what instrument it is. Ask the children to tell you how they recognised the instrument. Discuss the quality of sound it made.
♦ Tell the children that they are going to explore musical instrument sounds in more detail using percussion instruments as well as the instruments on the music CD-Rom. Explain that you want them to listen to the sounds the instruments make, describe the sounds, draw the instruments and record the sounds. Use some of the percussion instruments to demonstrate how to use musical and expressive language to describe the sounds it makes. Make sure they understand the terms used in Activity sheets 1 and 2.
♦ Ask the children to remind you how to use a tape recorder to record a sound – what things do they need to remember? What buttons do they need to press? How do they rewind and play back the sounds to listen to their recording?

 Group activities

Focus group – with the teacher

♦ Demonstrate how to search the CD-Rom to locate specific instruments. Remind the children how to use the menus, index and key word facilities of the program. Explain that the sounds of the instruments have been stored on the CD-Rom in a similar way to using a tape recorder. Demonstrate how to play the sound of the instruments. Ask the children to search for one instrument from the string family and one from the wind family. Ask them to draw and name the instrument, then use a tape recorder to make a recording of the sound. Ask them to write a description of the sound.

Using the photocopiable activity sheets

♦ The sheets can be completed before or after the computer session.

 Plenary session

Share the responses to the activity sheets. Ask someone from each group to play the recording of their instruments then discuss the children's descriptions. Does everyone agree? Are similar describing words used? Discuss any problems they may have had in using the tape recorder. Discuss the computer task. How difficult was it to locate the instruments and play the sounds? Listen to the children's recordings – can they match the sound to the pictures they have drawn? Which recording is clearer – percussion or the CD-Rom instruments? Why? What problems might there be in storing the sounds on a tape recorder compared to a CD-Rom? Which one produces a higher quality of reproduction?

✦ Percussion instruments ✦

✦ Complete this table by playing and listening carefully to the instruments listed.

Instrument	Description of sound it makes Put a ✔						Drawing of instrument
	dull	metallic	wooden	bright	mellow	harsh	
drum							
triangle							
xylophone							
sleigh bells							

✦ Now use a tape recorder to record the sound of each instrument.

✦ Percussion instruments ✦

✦ Complete this table by playing and listening carefully to the instruments listed. Use the words in the box as well as your own to write your descriptions.

harsh	mellow	soft	metallic	wooden
hollow	tapping	rattling	clear	muffled

Instrument	Description of sound it makes	Drawing of instrument
tambourine		
cymbal		
castanets		
maraca		

✦ Now use a tape recorder to record the sound of each instrument.

Photocopiable
©Hopscotch Educational Publishing

✦ Percussion instruments ✦

✦ Complete this table by playing and listening carefully to the instruments listed. Use the words in the box to write your descriptions. Use a dictionary to look up the meaning of any words you do not know.

resonant	grating	mellow	harsh	wooden
metallic	tinkling	smooth	clashing	bright

Instrument	Description of sound it makes	Drawing of instrument
cabassa		
tambour		
Indian bells		
wood blocks		

✦ Now use a tape recorder to record the sound of each instrument.

Lesson 6

Making music

Learning objectives

◆ To explore, create, select, combine and organise sounds.
◆ To understand that ICT can be used to organise and reorganise sounds.
◆ To use icons in a music composition computer program to arrange musical phrases.

Resources

◆ Photocopiable pages 60 and 61.
◆ Tape recorders.
◆ Percussion instruments.
◆ Music composition software.

Whole class introduction

◆ Photocopy pages 60 and 61 onto card and cut out the individual cards. Tell the children that they will be making some music today using percussion instruments as well as a computer program. Tell them that it is possible for them to 'write' some music without using the traditional musical notation. Show them one of the cards from pages 60 or 61. Ask them to look at the card and tell you what they think they would do with a drum or xylophone in order to 'read' this card. For example, card 1 could be single hits on a drum for: 1 hit – pause – 1hit – pause – 1 hit – 2 hits – pause – 1 hit. Card 2 might start off as a quiet sound then build to a loud sound, then fade away again. Explore the ideas the children suggest.
◆ Next, put all the cards out in any order and play the music for each card as one continuous piece of music. Ask the children to put up their hand when they think you have changed to a new card. Change the order of the cards – how does this change the music? Which order do they like best? Why? Try playing the music with different instruments – which one sounds best? Why?
◆ Play a different phrase with an instrument. Ask the children to invent their own symbol for this. Share ideas and write the symbols on the board. Explain that in writing the symbol and playing the music they are actually composing their own pieces of music. Tell them that they will be carrying out this

task themselves in groups using percussion instruments and symbol cards. Explain that they will also have the opportunity to create music in a similar way using a computer program.

Group activities

Focus group – with the teacher

◆ Demonstrate how an icon in a music composition program represents a musical phrase. Play each phrase. Ask the children to describe the sounds – are they happy/sad?, fast/slow?, harsh/mellow? If they were drawing symbols for the sounds how might they draw them? Demonstrate how to select icons to make a musical sequence.
◆ Re-arrange the same icons in a different sequence – how does it compare with the first one? Which one sounds better? Why? Ask the children to work in pairs or as a group to create their own musical sequence and save it to share later.

Using the photocopiable activity sheets

◆ Use the activity sheets before the computer program.

Plenary session

Ask each group to display their symbol cards in order and play the recording of their music. Can the others work out when the sounds change for each card? What do they think of the final performance? Do they like the choice of instruments? Compare this activity with using the computer program. Was this easier or more difficult to do? Why? Listen to the children's computer sequences. What differences can they notice between computer-controlled sounds and those produced by percussion instruments? What advantages/ disadvantages are there in using a computer to compose music?

✦ **Making music** ✦

✦ Cut out the symbol cards below. Make up your own musical symbol for the blank card. Arrange the symbols to create a piece of music using percussion instruments.

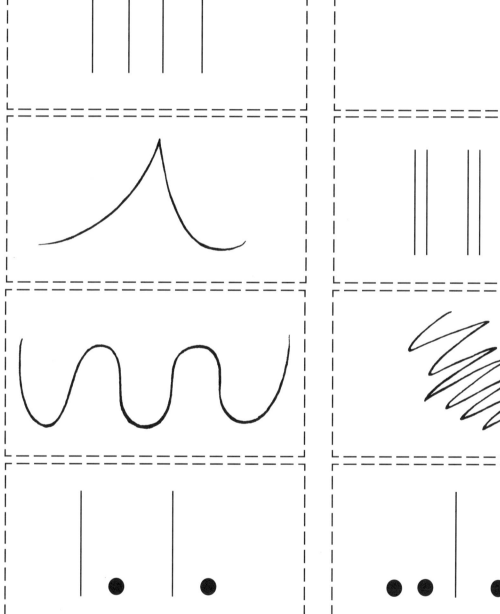

✦ Making music ✦

✦ Cut out the symbol cards below. Make up your own musical symbol for the blank cards. Arrange the symbols to create a piece of music using percussion instruments.

Photocopiable

©Hopscotch Educational Publishing

✦ Making music ✦

✦ Cut out the symbol cards below. Make up your own musical symbol for the blank cards. Arrange the symbols to create a piece of music using percussion instruments.

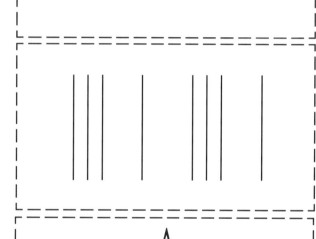

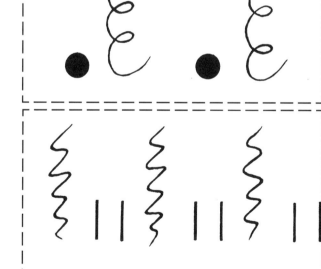

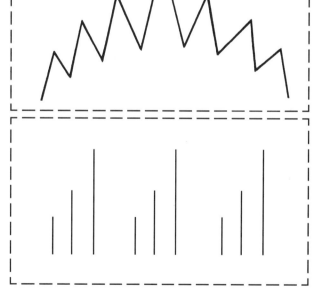

Databases – introduction

Learning objectives

+ To understand that collecting and storing information in an organised way helps us to find specific information.
+ To know that information on record cards is divided into fields and that a set of record cards is called a file.
+ To understand that information can be held as numbers, words or fixed choices, sometimes known as key words.

Resources

+ Photocopiable pages 62 and 63.
+ Some information books about the sea.
+ An enlarged version of one of the records on page 62.

Whole class activities

+ Photocopy pages 62 and 63 (enough for each child or pair to have a copy of both pages). Cut out the cards and put them into envelopes.
+ Show the children books about the sea and ask them how they might be able to find information about a particular sea animal, such as a blue whale. Which book would they look in first? Why? Where would they look in the book? Why? Remind them about the contents and index pages.
+ Explain that to find out very specific information about an animal, such as what colour it is and what it eats, they might have to look in several books because not all books have the same information about an animal. Say that if the information in all the books was organised in some way it would be easier to find what we want.
+ Tell the children that you are going to show them a way of organising a lot of information. They will be using a set of records, called a file to find information. Use the enlarged version of a record card from page 62 to demonstrate what a record is. Explain how each card in the file contains information about one sea animal, divided into separate headings, called fields. Point to and name each field. Explain that each record in the file they will be using has the same fields. Ask

questions related to the fields, such as 'What information is in the limbs field?' Explain how the information collected can be presented in different ways in each field, for example as a number in the 'limbs' and 'length' fields, as a choice (yes or no) in the 'fins' and 'teeth' fields or in words as in the other fields. (Explain that the length given is the maximum length, the colour and food are the main ones for each animal and limbs refer to legs, flippers and wings.)

+ Provide each child or pair with their envelope of records and ask them to take them out and put them in a pile. Ask them to imagine that if the cards were put into a file box like a filing cabinet (hence the name 'file'), they could flip through the cards to find the information they wanted. Discuss the advantages of having cards with all the same information on them (fields) all together in a file, compared with using a collection of information books.
+ Next ask the children to use the cards to answer questions like those on the activity sheets. For example, 'Which record has information about the whale shark?', 'What information is on record 5 in the food field?' Make sure they understand the terms 'file', 'record' and 'field' and are confident in answering questions about the records before using the activity sheets. (Note: the Beluga whales' tail flukes are classified as fins and their flippers as limbs.)

Group activities

Activity sheets

+ Use the sheets for group work after the whole class activities. Make sure the children realise that the answers might be 'no record'.

Plenary session

Compare answers. How easy was it to find the information they required? What uses could they see for a file on sea animals? What is something new they have learned today?

✦ Sea animals ✦

✦ Use the record cards below to answer the questions.

1 	**Name:** green sea turtle **Animal type:** reptile
Length: 1.0 m **Colour:** green **Fins:** no	**Limbs:** 4 **Teeth:** no **Food:** plants

2 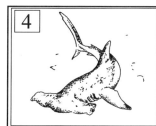	**Name:** fulmar **Animal type:** bird
Length: 0.47m **Colour:** grey **Fins:** no	**Limbs:** 4 **Teeth:** no **Food:** fish

3 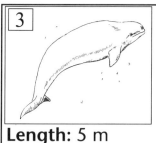	**Name:** beluga whale **Animal type:** mammal
Length: 5 m **Colour:** white **Fins:** yes	**Limbs:** 2 **Teeth:** yes **Food:** fish

4	**Name:** hammerhead shark **Animal type:** fish
Length: 4 m **Colour:** grey **Fins:** yes	**Limbs:** 0 **Teeth:** yes **Food:** fish

✦ Put a ✔ in the correct box to answer these questions:

1. How many records are on this page?   2 ☐ 4 ☐
2. Which record has information about the beluga whale?   2 ☐ 3 ☐
3. How many fields are there on each record card?   6 ☐ 8 ☐
4. What information is in the following fields?
   - a) record 2, limbs field   4 ☐ 2 ☐
   - b) record 4, length field   4m ☐ 5m ☐
   - c) record 1, animal type field   reptile ☐ fish ☐
   - d) record 3, colour field   brown ☐ white ☐
   - e) record 4, name field   hammerhead shark ☐ fulmar ☐

✦ Sea animals ✦

✦ Use the record cards below to answer the questions.

1		**Name:** green sea turtle

Name: green sea turtle

Animal type: reptile

Length: 1.0 m   **Limbs:** 4
Colour: green   **Teeth:** no
Fins: no   **Food:** plants

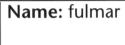

2

Name: fulmar

Animal type: bird

Length: 0.47m   **Limbs:** 4
Colour: grey   **Teeth:** no
Fins: no   **Food:** fish

3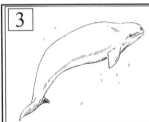

Name: beluga whale

Animal type: mammal

Length: 5 m   **Limbs:** 2
Colour: white   **Teeth:** yes
Fins: yes   **Food:** fish

4

Name: hammerhead shark

Animal type: fish

Length: 4 m   **Limbs:** 0
Colour: grey   **Teeth:** yes
Fins: yes   **Food:** fish

✦ Answer these questions:

1. How many records are on this page? _____

2. Which record has information about the beluga whale?

_____

3. How many fields are there on each record card? _____

4. What information is in the following fields?

    a) record 2, limbs field _____

    b) record 4, length field _____

    c) record 1, animal type field _____

    d) record 3, colour field _____

    e) record 4, name field _____

    f) record 2, food field _____

    g) record 1, fins field _____

ICT Skills

Photocopiable
©Hopscotch Educational Publishing

✦ Sea animals ✦

✦ Use the record cards below to answer the questions.

<table>
<tr>
<td>

1

Length: 1.0 m
Colour: green
Fins: no

</td>
<td>

Name: green sea turtle

Animal type: reptile

Limbs: 4
Teeth: no
Food: plants

</td>
<td>

2

Length: 0.47m
Colour: grey
Fins: no

</td>
<td>

Name: fulmar

Animal type: bird

Limbs: 4
Teeth: no
Food: fish

</td>
</tr>
<tr>
<td>

3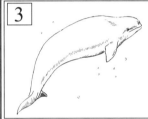

Length: 5 m
Colour: white
Fins: yes

</td>
<td>

Name: beluga whale

Animal type: mammal

Limbs: 2
Teeth: yes
Food: fish

</td>
<td>

4

Length: 4 m
Colour: grey
Fins: yes

</td>
<td>

Name: hammerhead shark

Animal type: fish

Limbs: 0
Teeth: yes
Food: fish

</td>
</tr>
</table>

✦ Answer these questions:

1. How many records contain information about fish? _____

2. Which record has information about the beluga whale? _____

3. How many fields are there on each record card? _____

4. What information is in the following fields?

    a) record 2, limbs field _____

    b) record 4, length field _____

    c) record 1, animal type field _____

5. Which record(s) has the following information?

    a) limbs field – 4 _____

    b) colour field – brown _____

    c) food field – fish _____

Lesson 8

Databases – adding records

 Learning objectives

✦ To extract relevant information to complete a record card.
✦ To know that information can be taken from pictures or text.
✦ To understand that ICT can be used to store and sort information.
✦ To add a record to a file in a computer database.

 Resources

✦ Envelopes of record cards from lesson 7.
✦ Activity sheet 3 from Lesson 3 (page 17).
✦ A colour picture of a bottle-nose dolphin.
✦ A computer database.

 Whole class introduction

✦ Before the lesson, write out (or enlarge on a photocopier) the information about dolphins from the top part of Activity sheet 3 (page 17).
✦ Remind the children about what they did in Lesson 7. Can they tell you what a file, record and field are? Tell them that they are going to write their own record card and you will show them how to do this. Put the dolphin picture and the text where all the children can see them. Remind them of the fields used in the record cards: name, animal type, length, limbs, colour, fins, food and teeth. Write these on the board. Explain that they are going to use the picture and the text to find the information they need for each field.
✦ Share the text. Ask them to tell you if it contains any information needed to complete a record about bottle-nose dolphins. Underline the key words in the text, such as mammal, bottle-nose dolphin, 3 metres, teeth and fish. Write this information in the correct fields.
✦ Ask the children what information is missing. Say that they can also use pictures or illustrations to obtain information. Look at the picture together and ask them to use it to complete the fields for colour, limbs and fins.
✦ Tell them that they will now write their own record card in a similar way by using an activity sheet.

Explain that you will also be showing them how a computer can be used to store a file of records.
✦ It is important that they complete the sheets before working with you on the computer.

 Group activities

Focus group – with the teacher

✦ Prepare a database with the same fields as the sea animals records. Tell the children what a database is and how it can contain exactly the same information as the record cards they have been using. Remind them how they had to search through their paper cards to find the answers to questions in Lesson 7. Say that the computer program is designed to do this for them much more quickly!
✦ Demonstrate how to open the program and select the correct file on sea animals. Show them how to add a record to the database, making sure they are aware that they must spell the words they enter correctly or the computer will not recognise what it means. Ask them to work as a small group or in pairs to enter a record. They could be assigned a record each from those on pages 62 and 63.

Using the photocopiable activity sheets

✦ Use the sheets before the computer session.

Plenary session

Share the answers to the activity sheets. Which fields could be gleaned from the picture? Which from the text? What similarities are there in preparing a written record with that of a computer record? What advantages and disadvantages are there in using a written record compared with a computer file?

✦ Making a record ✦

✦ Use the picture and the writing below to complete
   the record card.

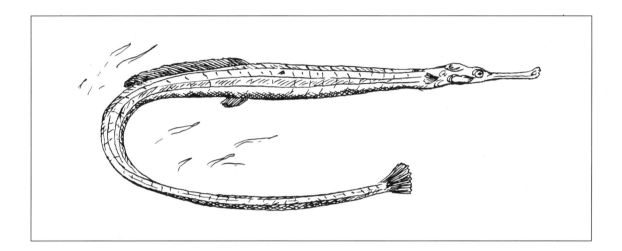

The great pipefish is a fish that likes to live in seaweed.
It has a very long, thin body.
It can grow up to 50 cm in length.
It is brown in colour and has darker markings on it.
The great pipefish has no teeth. It eats crustaceans.

Name: _____
Animal type: _____

Length: _____   Limbs: _____
Colour: _____
Fins: _____   Teeth: _____
Food: _____

✦ Making a record ✦

✦ Use the picture and the writing below to complete the record card.

Atlantic salmon are fish that spend most of their lives in the sea but return to rivers to have their young.

The baby salmon live for up to four years in the river and then they swim to the sea. At this stage they turn a silvery colour and are called smolts.

The adult salmon can grow up to 100cm in length and can weigh 30kg.

Atlantic salmon use their teeth to eat the small fish they catch.

Name: _____

Animal type: _____

Length: _____   Limbs: _____

Colour: _____

Fins: _____   Teeth: _____

Food: _____

ICT Skills

✦ Making a record ✦

✦ Use the picture and the writing below to complete the record card.

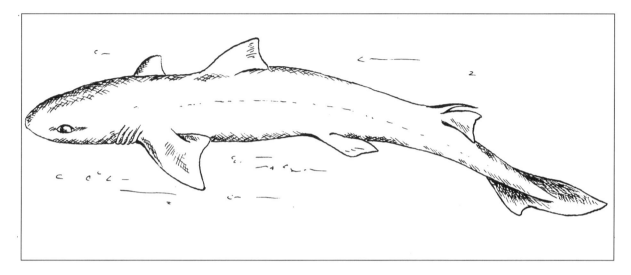

The spiny dogfish is a very streamlined fish that can reach lengths of 1 metre. The mouth is equipped with rows of very sharp teeth adapted for holding and tearing the small fish it eats as prey. The dogfish has five gill slits on the side of its body through which oxygen is absorbed from the water. The skin is very coarse and feels like sandpaper. The colour of the fish helps to camouflage it because the ventral (under) side is silver to look like the silvery surface of the water as seen from below and the dorsal (top) side is brown to look like the bottom of the sea as seen from above.

Name: _____

Animal type: _____

Length: _____   Limbs: _____

Colour: _____

Fins: _____   Teeth: _____

Food: _____

Databases – searching

 Learning objectives

✦ To answer simple questions about a file by ordering records by a key field.
✦ To search a computer database to answer simple questions.

 Resources

✦ Record cards from Lesson 7.
✦ A computer database.

 Whole class introduction

✦ Remind the children of the records they have been using about sea animals and how they previously entered the information on the records into the computer database program. Tell them that they will now be learning how to use the computer to answer questions about the file, but before they do that, you will be showing them how to search the paper record cards so that they can understand how the computer comes up with the answers to the questions.

✦ Select 16 children and give them one record card each. Ask them to stand out in front of the class in card number order. Tell the others to imagine that these children are now inside the computer because someone has entered their records into the database program. Explain that now the records are inside the computer we can use them to find the answers to questions we may have. For example, we may want to know how many of the sea animals in our file are mammals. (Stress that the database can contain only information entered into it, it cannot contain information about <u>all</u> sea animals unless they have been added to the file.) Say that in order to find the answer to this question, they need to know which field to search – in this case it is animal type – so the way to search the file is: animal type field = mammal. Ask the children to look at their cards in the animal type field and put their hand up if their card says mammal. These children then step forward. Explain that the computer would search as they did and then select the records with

mammal. Ask the children to read out the names of the sea animals that are mammals.

✦ Repeat this many times using different questions, some of which involve ordering, such as: 'Which sea animal is the longest?' (Order by field length – ask the children to order themselves according to length.) They will be able to see that manually sorting in this way takes time. Explain that the value of using the computer to search the file is that it can do it much more quickly. Make sure they realise that sometimes the answer will be 'no record', for example with 'colour field = green'.

✦ The children will need to do the sheets before working with the teacher at the computer. (Note: the tail flukes of the whale are classified as fins.)

 Group activities

Focus group – with the teacher

✦ Show the children how to use the database program to search the file. You may want to use the same questions you used with the paper records to see if the computer comes up with the same answers! Then ask the children to work in pairs or as a small group to answer some more questions.
Note: after each search make sure the children select 'all the records' to ensure they are back to using the whole set of records again.

Using the photocopiable activity sheets

✦ Use the sheets before the computer session. Note that in Activity 3 the children need to realise that some questions may require a zero answer.

 Plenary session

Share answers for the activity sheets and computer questions. Discuss any problems the children may have had and how they solved them. Discuss the advantages and disadvantages of using the computer to do the searching.

✦ Searching records ✦

✦ Use the record cards below to answer the questions.

 **1**

Name: sea lion

Animal type: mammal

Length: 2.2m   **Limbs:** 4
Colour: brown   **Teeth:** yes
Fins: no   **Food:** fish

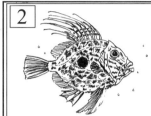 **2**

Name: John Dory

Animal type: fish

Length: 0.40m   **Limbs:** 0
Colour: many   **Teeth:** no
Fins: yes   **Food:** fish

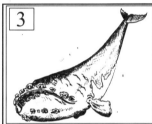 **3**

Name: right whale

Animal type: mammal

Length: 18m   **Limbs:** 2
Colour: black   **Teeth:** no
Fins: yes   **Food:** plankton

 **4**

Name: spiny squat lobster

Animal type: crustacean

Length: 0.12m   **Limbs:** 10
Colour: orange   **Teeth:** no
Fins: no   **Food:** debris*

* Debris = dead plant and animal matter

✦ Put a ✔ in the correct box to answer these questions:

1. What is the longest animal?   right whale ☐   lobster ☐
2. How many animals are mammals?   2 ☐   3 ☐
3. Which animal has teeth?   right whale ☐   sea lion ☐
4. What is the shortest animal?   lobster ☐   John Dory ☐
5. Which animal eats plankton?   right whale ☐   sea lion ☐
6. Which animal is a fish?   lobster ☐   John Dory ☐

◆ Searching records ◆

✦ Use the record cards below to answer the questions.

1

Name: sea lion

Animal type: mammal

Length: 2.2m
Colour: brown
Fins: no

Limbs: 4
Teeth: yes
Food: fish

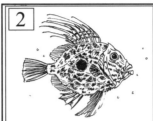

2

Name: John Dory

Animal type: fish

Length: 0.40m
Colour: many
Fins: yes

Limbs: 0
Teeth: no
Food: fish

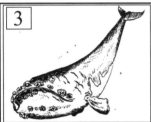

3

Name: right whale

Animal type: mammal

Length: 18m
Colour: black
Fins: yes

Limbs: 2
Teeth: no
Food: plankton

4

Name: spiny squat lobster

Animal type: crustacean

Length: 0.12m
Colour: orange
Fins: no

Limbs: 10
Teeth: no
Food: debris*

* Debris = dead plant and animal matter

✦ Answer these questions:

1. What is the longest animal? _____

2. Which animals are mammals? _____

3. Which animals do not have teeth? _____

4. What is the shortest animal? _____

5. Which animals eat fish? _____

6. Which animals are fish? _____

7. Which animals have fins? _____

8. Which animal is brown? _____

ICT
Skills

✦ Searching records ✦

✦ Use the record cards below to answer the questions.

Name: sea lion

Animal type: mammal

Length: 2.2m **Limbs:** 4
Colour: brown **Teeth:** yes
Fins: no **Food:** fish

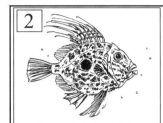

Name: John Dory

Animal type: fish

Length: 0.40m **Limbs:** 0
Colour: many **Teeth:** no
Fins: yes **Food:** fish

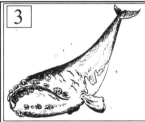

Name: right whale

Animal type: mammal

Length: 18m **Limbs:** 2
Colour: black **Teeth:** no
Fins: yes **Food:** plankton

Name: spiny squat lobster

Animal type: crustacean

Length: 0.12m **Limbs:** 10
Colour: orange **Teeth:** no
Fins: no **Food:** debris*

* Debris = dead plant and animal matter

✦ Answer these questions:

1. Order the animals in length from the longest to the shortest.

   _____

2. Which animal has teeth?_____

3. Which animals are shorter than 1 metre?_____

4. Which animals are mammals?_____

5. Which animals eat fish?_____

6. Which animals are longer than 1 metre? _____

7. Which animals have more than 10 limbs?_____

8. Which animals have no teeth?_____

Lesson 10

Databases – bar charts

Learning objectives

✦ To use a bar chart to represent information.
✦ To interpret information in a bar chart.
✦ To use a computer database to generate bar charts and interpret the data produced.

Resources

✦ Record cards from Lesson 7, pages 62 and 63.
✦ A computer database.

Whole class introduction

✦ Remind the children how they used records in a file to answer questions in Lesson 9. Tell them that today they will be learning another way of representing information contained in the file.
✦ Provide each child or pair with the envelope of paper record cards. Ask them to sort the cards into piles, according to animal type. Then ask them to count how many cards are in each pile. Draw a table on the board to show the result:

animal	mammal	fish	bird	reptile	mollusc	echinoderm	crustacean
number	3	6	2	1	2	1	1

✦ Explain that this information could now be presented as a bar chart. Model how to draw the bar chart, showing the children how to number the vertical axis in ones and how to label the horizontal axis. Remind them that the graph also needs a title and ask them to suggest what this might be.

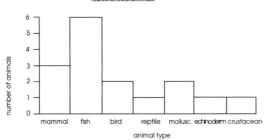

✦ Ask questions about the bar chart, such as: 'What is this bar chart about?', 'How many sea animals in our file are mammals?', 'Which animal type

has the most animals?', 'Which has the fewest animals?','Which animal type has more than five animals in it?'
✦ Tell the children that they will now be using an activity sheet to do some bar charts of their own and that you will also be showing them how to use the computer to make bar charts.
✦ It is important that the children complete the activity sheets before working on the computer.

Group activities

Focus group – with the teacher

✦ Tell the children that the database program is capable of producing bar charts. Explain that it sorts through the records in the file in a similar way to the way they manually sorted the paper record cards and it then presents a bar chart. Show them how to produce a bar chart of animal types so they can compare it with the one produced earlier in class.
✦ Ask them to work in pairs or a small group to produce a bar chart of their own. Ask them to print it out and write a sentence about it to show that they understand the graph.
Note: you can paste a graph into a word processing program just like any other graphic.

Using the photocopiable activity sheets

✦ Use the sheets before the computer session.

Plenary session

Ask the children to share their bar charts from the activity sheets and the computer. Share answers to the questions and ask some children to read out their sentence about the computer produced chart. Compare the hand and computer completed bar charts - what advantages and disadvantages are there in using a computer to do this task?

✦ Bar charts ✦

✦ Use the table below to complete this bar chart.
   Colour it in.

food	fish	plankton	jellyfish	molluscs	crustaceans
number of animals	6	6	1	2	1

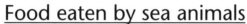

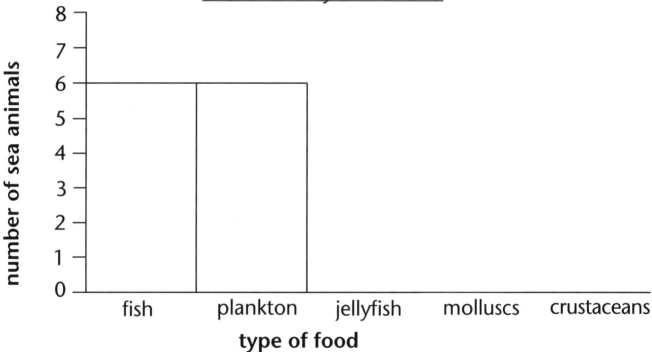

Food eaten by sea animals

✦ Answer these questions:

  1. How many sea animals eat molluscs?_____

  2. How many sea animals eat fish?_____

  3. How many sea animals eat plankton?_____

  4. How many types of food are eaten?_____

✦ Bar charts ✦

✦ Use the sea creature record cards to complete this table. Then complete and colour the bar chart. Colour it in.

colour	brown	grey	silver	white	black	orange	blue	many
number of animals	3							

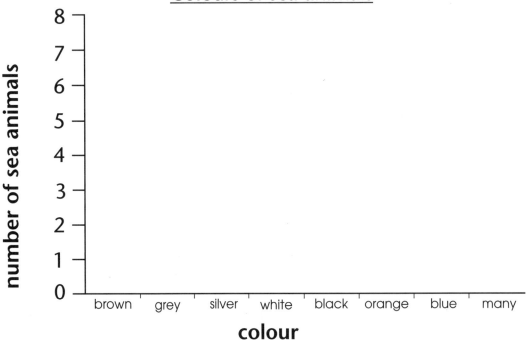

Colours of sea animals

✦ Answer these questions:

1. What does the bar chart show us?_____

_____

2. How many sea animals are silver?_____

3. How many sea animals are grey?_____

4. What is the most common colour of the sea animals in these records?_____

5. What colours are least common?_____

ICT Skills

✦ Bar charts ✦

✦ Use the sea animal record cards to complete this table. Then draw a bar chart to present the information. Colour it in.

length	less than 1 metre	1 to 5 metres	6 to 10 metres	11 to 15 metres	over 16 metres
number of animals					

✦ Draw your bar chart here. Give it a title.

✦ Answer these questions:

1. What does the bar chart show us?_____

   _____

2. How many sea animals are over 15 metres?_____

3. What is the most common length of the sea animals in these records?_____

4. How many animals are between 1 and 15 metres long?_____

Lesson 11

Simulations

 Learning objectives

- ✦ To understand that computer simulations can represent real or imaginary situations.
- ✦ To understand that computer simulations can allow users to explore options.
- ✦ To enter data in a computer simulation and discuss the consequences of options.
- ✦ To evaluate a computer simulation.

 Resources

- ✦ A computer simulation that allows the user to make choices, enter data and explore consequences.

 Whole class introduction

- ✦ Explain to the children that they will be using a computer simulation program. Discuss the term 'simulation' to define its meaning. Ask them if they have ever used a computer simulation before, for example in an amusement arcade. Can they think of examples where computer simulations might be very useful – for training aeroplane pilots, designing buildings and so on? Tell them that simulations allow us to experience situations that might otherwise be dangerous (such as in testing products), impossible (such as exploring a past period in time or an imaginary world) or not practical (such as visiting a foreign country). Talk about how using these kinds of programs allow us to experience things we might otherwise never be able to experience.

 Group activities

Focus group – with the teacher

- ✦ Demonstrate the main features of the program. Show the children how to make choices and enter data. Ask them to tell you how a computer simulation is different from a video – stress that it is interactive, not passive. Tell them that a computer simulation is limited to a certain number of choices – the choices are not infinite! Ask them to predict the kinds of things they think they may experience when using the program. What kinds of things might they have to do? Ask them to explore the first part of the simulation and to record any decisions they make and the results of their decisions.

Using the photocopiable activity sheets

- ✦ Use the sheets after the children have completed the simulation.

 Plenary session

Bring the whole class together again when they have all completed their activity sheets and have used the computer simulation. Ask the children to share their recordings of what decisions they made and what happened. Discuss the different consequences of different actions. What happens when you try this option? Does it always happen? Discuss any patterns and connections they have identified and talk about how they could test these to see if they are always true. Share the evaluation sheets. How useful do they think the simulation is? How does it compare with others they have used at home or at school? What did they like/ dislike about the program? How do they think it could be improved?

✦ Computer program review ✦

Program_____

Publisher_____

✦ Circle your answers about this program:

1. Do you like this program?	yes	no
2. Is the program easy to use?	yes	no
3. Is the program about real or imaginary things?	real	imaginary
4. Can you make choices when using this program?	yes	no
5. Do you think you made good choices?	yes	no
6. Does the program help you learn things?	yes	no
7. Would you do things differently if you used the program again?	yes	no
8. Would you recommend the program to others?	yes	no

✦ Answer these questions:

1. Write down what you like about this program.

_____

_____

_____

_____

2. Write down what you do not like about this program.

_____

_____

_____

Name _____ **Activity 2** **Date** _____

✦ Computer program review ✦

Program_____ Publisher_____

✦ Answer these questions:

1. Do you like using this program? Why/why not? _____

_____

2. Is the program about real or imaginary things? _____

3. Can you make choices when using this program? _____

4. Write about a good choice you made and what happened.

_____

_____

_____

5. What have you learned from using the program? _____

_____

_____

6. Write down what you like about this program. _____

_____

_____

_____

7. Write down how you think this program could be improved.

_____

Photocopiable
©Hopscotch Educational Publishing

✦ Computer program review ✦

Program_____ Publisher_____

✦ Answer the following questions:

1. Briefly explain what the program is about. _____

   _____

2. How realistic is it? _____

   _____

   _____

3. What do you think the program helps you learn about?

   _____

   _____

4. Describe a decision you made in the program and what
   happened.

   _____

   _____

   _____

5. How does this program compare with others you have used?

   _____

   _____

6. How do you think the program could be improved?

   _____

   _____

Lesson 12

e-mail

Learning objectives

- To understand that messages can be sent over distances.
- To write a letter.
- To know that ICT can be used to send messages.
- To receive and reply to e-mails.

Resources

- A computer with e-mail facility and internet access.

Whole class introduction

- Tell the children that they will be learning about sending messages. Ask them to tell you some of the ways they know that messages can be sent today or in the past. List them on the board. Include carrier pigeon, smoke signals, signalling flags, morse code, letter, radio, telephone, telegrams and fax.
- Ask them to think about the advantages and disadvantages of each one on the list. Consider speed, convenience, confidentiality, permanence and cost.
- Explain that the most common form of sending messages is letter writing. Ask them to consider how letter writing has changed over time. Discuss how computers have changed many people's letter writing habits from a handwritten response to a wordprocessed one. Explain how once the letter has been wordprocessed it can be sent by fax, e-mail or in the traditional way by post. Which method do the children consider to be best? Why? Does the method used depend on the type of letter to be sent? Would you send a business letter in the same way as a personal letter, for example?
- Tell the children that they are going to write their own letter and then compare this with sending an e-mail using the computer.
- Model how to write a personal letter on the board before they use the activity sheets. Talk about how a letter can begin and end.
  Note: the children should do the activity sheets before working with the teacher on the computer.

Group activities

Focus group – with the teacher

- Ask a teacher at another school to let their class send you some e-mails. Show the children how to open the mail box and read the messages. Show them how to reply to the e-mail. Point out that when using e-mail people are usually more casual and do not use 'dear' and 'yours sincerely' and so on. There is a different etiquette, for example you must always enter a line saying what the subject of your e-mail is because this helps the receiver to sort their mail. Ask the children to open an e-mail, read it and reply to it. Note: you may want to begin by having an e-mail address for the class rather than for each child. Explain that no two addresses are the same and they all tend to use lower case letters. Give them an address, such as paul_opler@usqs.gov – this is a useful address as Dr Paul Opler is a world expert on butterflies and the children could e-mail questions to him. Explain that the part before @ (said 'at') refers to a specific user and the part after @ refers to the service that handles their e-mail. There are certain e-mail packages (such as excitepost) that prevent children receiving messages from anyone not in their address book. It is not advisable to allow primary-aged children to use e-mail without supervision because it is as open to abuse as the passing of any other messages.

Using the photocopiable activity sheets

- Use the sheets before using the computer.

Plenary session

Share the handwritten letters. Compare hand writing a letter with writing an e-mail on the computer. Which is easier? Why? How do they differ? What different approaches/etiquette are used? Which one would the children rather receive? Why? What advantages and disadvantages are there of both methods?

✦ My letter ✦

✦ Imagine you are writing a letter to a pen pal. Complete the letter below by using your own words or words from the box.

Dear _____ ,

My name is _____. I am _____ years old. I live in _____. The names of the people in my family are _____

_____.

My favourite colour is _____. My favourite food is _____ and my favourite tv programme is_____.

The sport I like playing or watching best is _____

_____.

At school I like _____ best. My favourite animal is a _____.

Please write back soon,

Love from

✎ Write your own address or school address here. Write the date underneath.

✎ Sign your name

seven	eight	nine	blue	green	yellow	orange	purple
curry	spaghetti	roast	salad	fruit	beans	chips	burger
football	netball	cricket	rugby	swimming	art	writing	music

✦ My letter ✦

✦ Imagine you are writing a letter to a pen pal. Complete the following letter in your own words. Use a dictionary to help you.

Write your own address or school address here. Write the date underneath.

Dear _____ ,

My name is _____ . I am _____

_____

_____

_____ .

My favourite foods are:_____

_____ .

The things I enjoy doing most are: _____

_____ .

At school I like doing these things best:_____

_____ .

My favourite animals are:_____

_____ .

My favourite sports are:_____

_____ .

Please write soon,
Love from

Describe yourself – how old you are, what colour hair and eyes you have etc.

Sign your letter

ICT Skills

Photocopiable
©Hopscotch Educational Publishing

✦ My letter ✦

✦ Imagine you are writing a letter to a pen pal. Write about yourself – how old you are, what you look like, the people in your family, the things you like to do at home and at school. Use a dictionary to help you.

Don't forget to put your own or your school address in the top right-hand corner. Write the date underneath.

Dear _____ ,

Please write back soon,
Love from

◆ Appendix ◆

 Suggestions for using these pages...

Page 55

✦ This page is used with Lesson 1. You could enlarge it on a photocopier.
✦ Use the poem as a model for the children to write their own calligrams. Their handwritten and computer produced poems could be made into a class book.

Page 56

✦ This page is used with Lesson 2. You could enlarge it on a photocopier.
✦ Glue the page into a book and add the children's own wordprocessed endings to the story beginning to make a 'choose your own story' type of book.

Page 57

✦ This page is used with Lesson 3. You could enlarge it on a photocopier.
✦ The children could also use the page as a starting point to find out more information about sharks and whales by using a CD-Rom encyclopaedia.

Page 58

✦ This page is used with Lesson 4. You could enlarge it on a photocopier.
✦ The children could go on to make their own information book about ships and boats. They could use a CD-Rom encyclopaedia to find information.

Page 59

✦ This page is used with Lesson 5. You could enlarge it on a photocopier.
✦ Use the pictures to stimulate the children to find out about one or more instruments on the page.

Page 60

✦ This page is used with Lesson 6. Photocopy the page onto card for cutting out.

Page 61

✦ This page is used with Lesson 6. Photocopy the page onto card for cutting out.

Page 62

✦ This page is used with Lesson 7. Photocopy enough for each child or pair to have a copy of each page. Cut up the cards and put them into an envelope together with those on page 63.

Page 63

✦ This page is used with Lesson 7. Photocopy enough for each child or pair to have a copy of each page. Cut up the cards and put them into an envelope together with those on page 62.

Page 64

✦ This is an individual record sheet for recording the skills and knowledge achieved in ICT.

✦ Sea poems ✦

Creatures of the sea

Under the *waves* so **BIG** and blue

Live *FANTASTIC* creatures that will **amaze** you!

Like the `squidgy`  with **LONG** tentacle legs

And the **hard-shelled** oyster that lays **millions** of eggs.

There are  that can fly above the waves

And **fierce-looking** eels that **lurk** deep in caves

So make sure you look carefully before entering the *sea*

I don't want a shark's **teeth** to bite you or me!

The Cliff-top

The cliff-top has a carpet
    Of lilac, gold and green:
The blue sky bounds the ocean,
    The white clouds scud between.

A flock of gulls are wheeling
    And wailing round my seat;
Above my head the heaven,
    The sea beneath my feet.
              Robert Bridges

"What do you think it is?" asked Tamal.

"I don't know. Maybe it's buried treasure!" said an excited Anna.

The two children hurriedly scraped the sand away from the lid of the box and tried to open it.

"It must be locked. I can't open it!" cried Tamal in despair.

"Let's dig it out properly so we can see what we're doing," suggested Anna.

Together they used their spades to dig around the sides of the box and finally they managed to lift it out completely.

"It's so exciting," enthused Anna. "I can't wait to see what's inside!"

Tamal and Anna spent the next twenty minutes trying to open the lid of the box but it was no use, it was stuck fast.

i'm exhausted what are we going to do now tamal asked

do you think we can carry it to frank's garage i'm sure he'll be able to open it answered anna

great idea agreed tamal come on let's go

tamal and anna carried the box all the way along the beach to the car park where they stopped for a short rest soon they were at the garage

hello you two what have you got there   asked frank

we hope it's buried treasure said tamal we found it on the beach

buried treasure eh well we'll soon find out said frank as he broke the lock

well that's amazing he said as he looked inside the box

✦ Sharks and whales ✦

The shark

Sharks are large fish.

The shark's body is covered in rough scales.

They have sharp teeth.

Not all sharks are dangerous to man.

Sharks are fast swimmers.

The Hammerhead shark has a strange head like a hammer.

The Lemon shark has a yellowish underbelly.

The whale

Whales are <u>big</u> animals. In fact, the Blue Whale is probably the <u>biggest</u> animal ever to have lived. The body of the whale is covered in a <u>big</u> layer of blubber that helps it stay afloat as well as keeping it warm. Some whales have teeth. The teeth are <u>big</u>. Other whales have <u>big</u> structures known as baleen plates instead of teeth. When feeding these whales swim with their mouths open to catch the <u>big</u> number of plankton or krill which they live on.

large	gigantic	colossal	huge
immense	bulky	enormous	largest

✦ Ships and boats ✦

Hovercraft

A hovercraft is a vehicle that can travel over land, marshy ground or water. Fans make a cushion of air on which the hovercraft floats. There are propellers on deck to push the hovercraft forward.

Raft

A raft is a platform of logs, planks or oil drums that floats. Some rafts have sides and a sail. Rafts can be pushed along by oars or a pole.

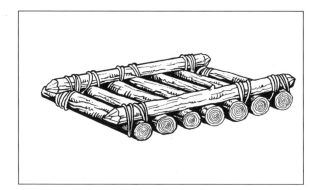

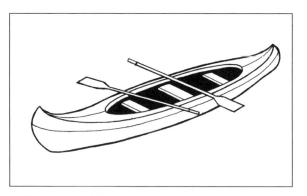

✦ Musical instruments ✦

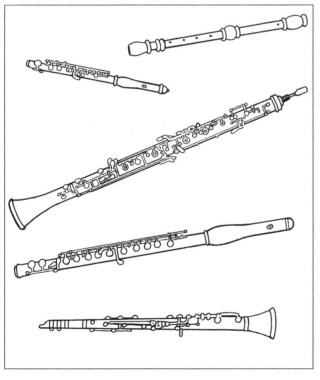

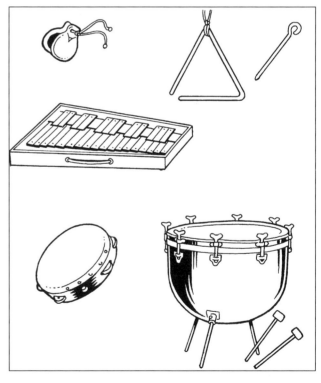

✦ Notation cards ✦

Card 2

Card 4

Card 1

Card 3

✦ Notation cards ✦

Card 6

Card 8

Card 5

Card 7

ICT Skills

Photocopiable
©Hopscotch Educational Publishing

61

✦ Record cards ✦

1	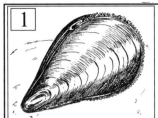	**Name:** mussel **Animal type:** mollusc

Length: 0.10m **Limbs:** 0
Colour: black **Teeth:** no
Fins: no **Food:** plankton

2		**Name:** grey seal **Animal type:** mammal

Length: 3m **Limbs:** 4
Colour: grey **Teeth:** yes
Fins: no **Food:** fish

3		**Name:** seahorse **Animal type:** fish

Length: 0.35m **Limbs:** 0
Colour: many **Teeth:** no
Fins: yes **Food:** plankton

4	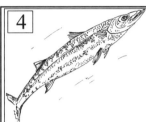	**Name:** barracuda **Animal type:** fish

Length: 1.8m **Limbs:** 0
Colour: silver **Teeth:** yes
Fins: yes **Food:** fish

5	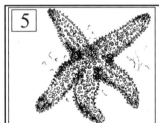	**Name:** common starfish **Animal type:** echinoderm

Length: 0.45m **Limbs:** 5
Colour: orange **Teeth:** no
Fins: no **Food:** molluscs

6		**Name:** fiddler crab **Animal type:** crustacean

Length: 0.04m **Limbs:** 10
Colour: many **Teeth:** no
Fins: no **Food:** plankton

7		**Name:** gannet **Animal type:** bird

Length: 0.90m **Limbs:** 4
Colour: white **Teeth:** no
Fins: no **Food:** fish

8		**Name:** cormorant **Animal type:** bird

Length: 0.90m **Limbs:** 4
Colour: brown **Teeth:** no
Fins: no **Food:** fish

✦ Record cards ✦

9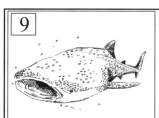

Name: whale shark

Animal type: fish

Length: 15m **Limbs:** 0
Colour: grey **Teeth:** yes
Fins: yes **Food:** plankton

10

Name: moray eel

Animal type: fish

Length: 3m **Limbs:** 0
Colour: many **Teeth:** yes
Fins: yes **Food:** fish

11

Name: sea otter

Animal type: mammal

Length: 1.2m **Limbs:** 4
Colour: brown **Teeth:** yes
Fins: no **Food:** molluscs

12

Name: blue whale

Animal type: mammal

Length: 30.5m **Limbs:** 2
Colour: grey **Teeth:** no
Fins: yes **Food:** plankton

13

Name: Atlantic cod

Animal type: fish

Length: 1.8m **Limbs:** 0
Colour: brown **Teeth:** yes
Fins: yes **Food:** fish

14

Name: blue damselfish

Animal type: fish

Length: 0.35m **Limbs:** 0
Colour: blue **Teeth:** no
Fins: yes **Food:** plankton

15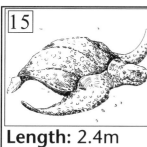

Name: leather-back turtle

Animal type: reptile

Length: 2.4m **Limbs:** 4
Colour: black **Teeth:** no
Fins: no **Food:** jellyfish

16

Name: common octopus

Animal type: mollusc

Length: 3m **Limbs:** 8
Colour: many **Teeth:** yes
Fins: no **Food:** crustaceans

ICT Skills
Year 3/P4

ICT Skills

Photocopiable

63

©Hopscotch Educational Publishing

Name_____ Year_____ Date_____ Level_____

Tick the boxes and look for best fit when assessing level.

QCA Expectations		QCA SOW Unit		NC level
some children will not have made so much progress and will:	combine graphics with text	3A	☐	
	use music software to create a sequence of musical phrases	3B	☐	
	enter data into a database with a predetermined structure and find information in it by matching the query to the question	3C	☐	2
	use simulations to make and test predictions; explore options	3D	☐	
	receive and reply to e-mails	3E	☐	
most children will:	combine graphics with text; use appropriate effects and re-size graphics	3A	☐	
	use music software to develop and refine a musical composition	3B	☐	
	enter data into a database with a predetermined structure and use it to answer straightforward questions and produce bar charts	3C	☐	3
	recognise patterns within simulations and make and test predictions	3D	☐	
	send, receive and reply to e-mails; develop and refine text messages	3E	☐	
some children will have progressed further and will:	combine graphics with text; choose effects that match their purposes so that the graphics and text complement each other	3A	☐	
	use music software to develop and refine a musical composition and adapt it in the light of performance	3B	☐	
	enter data into a database with a predetermined structure and use it to answer straightforward questions and produce bar charts; turn questions into search criteria	3C	☐	3-4
	identify the relationships and rules on which the simulations are based and test their predictions	3D	☐	
	send, receive and reply to e-mails; develop and refine text messages; send text and images as attachments	3E	☐	

ICT Skills